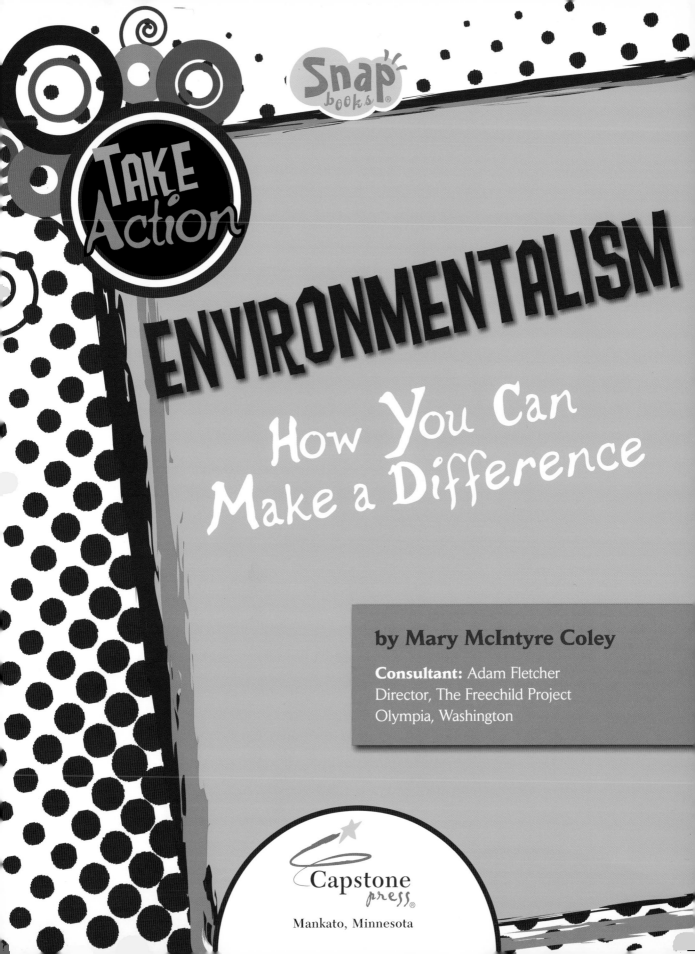

Snap books

Take Action

ENVIRONMENTALISM

How You Can Make a Difference

by Mary McIntyre Coley

Consultant: Adam Fletcher
Director, The Freechild Project
Olympia, Washington

Capstone press

Mankato, Minnesota

Snap Books are published by Capstone Press,
151 Good Counsel Drive, P.O. Box 669, Mankato, Minnesota 56002.
www.capstonepress.com

Library of Congress Cataloging-in-Publication Data
Coley, Mary McIntyre.
    Environmentalism : how you can make a difference / by Mary McIntyre Coley.
    p. cm. — (Snap books. Take action)
    Includes bibliographical references and index.
    Summary: "Describes what environmental activism is and serves as a guide explaining how youth can make change in
their world" — Provided by publisher.
    ISBN-13: 978-1-4296-2797-9 (hardcover)
    ISBN-10: 1-4296-2797-2 (hardcover)
    1. Environmentalism — Juvenile literature. 2. Environmentalists — Juvenile literature. I. Title.
GE195.5.C648 2009
333.72 — dc22   2008026946

Editor: Jennifer Besel
Designer: Veronica Bianchini
Photo Researcher: Wanda Winch
Photo shoot scheduler: Marcy Morin

Photo Credits: All photos by Capstone Press/Karon Dubke, except:
Courtesy of Adam Fletcher, 32 (bottom)
Courtesy of Otana Jakpor, 17
Courtesy of Tayler McGillis, 11
Courtesy of Zander Srodes, 25
Kids Saving the Rainforest/Marianne Coates, 5, 7
Photo courtesy of Mary Coley, 32 (top)
Save Our Stream, 21

Essential content terms are **bold** and are defined at the bottom of the page where they first appear.

1 2 3 4 5 6 14 13 12 11 10 09

Table of Contents

ONE TREE AT A TIME

Janine Licare lived in Manuel Antonio, Costa Rica. Her home was in the rain forest. She grew up seeing the tall trees, titi monkeys, and all the other wildlife in the tropical rain forest. But at the age of 9, Janine realized that the rain forest and all the animals that lived there were in danger. People were cutting down the trees for lumber. The land was being dug for farming. The rain forest was disappearing before her eyes. And in its place she saw roads, power lines, and machines.

Janine knew that the animals depended on the trees for a place to live. She also knew that people need trees too. Trees make the oxygen that all living things need to stay alive. Janine realized something had to be done to protect the rain forest.

But what could she do?

Janine Licare saw a problem in her world, and she decided to do something to change it.

Janine and her friend Aislin had previously raised money by selling painted rocks. They wanted to do something special with the money, but they weren't sure what. Then they thought about the rain forest that was being destroyed in their own backyards. The girls decided to put their money toward helping the rain forest. With the help of Janine's mom, the girls formed a club. They called themselves Kids Saving the Rainforest (KSTR).

To raise more money, Janine and Aislin opened a store in a local hotel. They sold artwork made by children. All the money they made went toward helping the animals or planting trees. And Janine set some high goals. Literally. One of KSTR's goals was to help the endangered titi monkey. Many monkeys were killed when they tried to use power lines to cross busy roads. Janine and her club raised money to build monkey bridges that cross above the roads. The idea helped the monkeys and got KSTR noticed.

Today Janine's club has members from all around the world. The club has built an education center to teach others about the rain forest and how they can help save it. Janine and other members have planted more than 4,000 trees. They set up an environmental library. And they have saved many young animals from death.

Janine and the other members of KSTR took action to help their environment. They know that kids can make a big difference.

Janine Licare

You Can Make a Difference Too!

An activist is someone who works to help make something better. Activists don't just complain about a problem. They do something about it. Environmentalists focus their work on helping nature.

There are hundreds of ways to be an environmental activist. As you begin, you might start small. Make changes in your home, neighborhood, or community. Then you can tackle global problems to change your country or even the world. Just like Janine, you can make a big difference. Ready to get started?

CHAPTER 2

FOCUSING IN

STEP 1: BRAINSTORM PROBLEMS

The first step is deciding what you want to improve. Think about the things you see every day. Maybe there's a lot of trash beside a nearby road. Does your dad throw soda cans in the trash? As you're thinking, grab a piece of paper and a pen. Start to brainstorm. Think about issues and write them down. Don't judge your ideas. And don't worry about how you'd fix the problem. You can do that later. Step 1 is all about gathering ideas.

Problems can be big or small, local or global. Think about issues you've heard about on the news. Question topics you covered in science class. Did any of those topics make you upset or frustrated? Maybe you're worried that polar bears might become extinct. If so, write that down. If you're concerned about air quality in your state, write that down too.

Rules and Laws

Local, state, and national governments have many laws that protect the environment. Some laws limit gasses that come out of cars. Other laws protect certain

animals. There are even laws that tell companies how to get rid of their waste products. Maybe your school has a policy about recycling. If you'd like to change a rule or law, add that to your list. Or if you think a new law should be made about something, mark that down too. There's no limit to your ideas.

Tip Sometimes ideas come slowly. Don't give up. Talk with your friends or family to see if they know of some environmental problems. Just talking about it often sparks a few new ideas.

BRAINSTORM IDEAS AND PICK A CAUSE

In step 1, you wrote down a bunch of problems. In step 2, you'll brainstorm some solutions to those problems. Write down small ideas, like putting a recycling bin in your kitchen. Write down your big ideas too. Big ideas could even include organizing a club, like Kids Saving the Rainforest.

Sometimes you might write down a problem that you think can't be solved. If that happens to you, try thinking about it in a different way. Write down ways that you could help make the problem better. Remember that big changes often come about because of lots of small actions.

Decide

After you have all your ideas on paper, read through your list. You have a lot of problems and solutions in front of you. Your task now is to pick which cause is best for you. You'll be spending a lot of time working on whatever you choose. Pick the idea that interests you most. Don't worry if you want to do more than one. You can always come back to this list later and tackle another item. You'll be changing the world one idea at a time.

When Tayler McGillis was 10 years old, he saw lots of aluminum cans piling up beside roads in his Illinois town. And nobody was doing anything about the trash. So Tayler set a goal. He decided to collect 500 pounds (227 kilograms) of aluminum by cleaning up the cans around town. With his mom's help, Tayler spent hours walking and collecting. But once Tayler met his goal, he didn't stop. Tayler realized that more work had to be done to keep the town clean. He asked businesses for help. With help, Tayler set up a drop center so people had a place to bring their cans. He also set up recycling bins in five nearby communities. To raise awareness, he spoke at schools and organizations about recycling. He even organized can drives to collect lots of cans.

In four years, Tayler collected more than 20,000 pounds (9,000 kilograms) of aluminum. Because of Tayler's action, his community and the environment are cleaner. And the money he raised from bringing in the aluminum went to a good cause. Tayler donated more than $7,000 to Habitat for Humanity and other charities.

Tayler McGillis

CHAPTER 3

KNOW YOUR STUFF

STEP 3: RESEARCH, RESEARCH, RESEARCH

Research is like a key. If you don't have it, you'll be locked outside. In order to make change, you have to know what's happening. You need to know who's in charge, why something is happening, or what has been done before. Step 3 is about becoming an expert on your topic. When you do get out there and start taking action, people will ask you questions. The media might want to interview you. You need to know facts and details about your issue. If you don't, it will be hard for people to believe in your cause.

Many People, Many Views

As you research, you will find that there are many different opinions. Consider the topic of recycling. One person might think it's needed to protect natural resources. Someone else may think recycling costs too much money. Another person may argue that making products from recycled material causes more pollution. Each person has a different point of view. And all people have their own reasons for believing as they do. When you come across opinions that are different from your own, be respectful. Even if you don't agree, opinions are not right or wrong. Try to understand different opinions. With that understanding, you'll be able to make a stronger case for change.

Even your family and friends might feel differently from you. That could be upsetting. But keep an open mind as you listen to their points. It is good to listen to other points of view. And if something they say changes your mind, that's all right too.

Get that Library Card

Gathering information can be a little overwhelming at first. Where do you even begin? A great place to start is the library. The library has access to all kinds of information that you don't have at home. Local librarians can help you find information about your topic. They will be able to help you find books, magazines, newspapers, or DVDs. Once you get the resources, dig in. Read or watch everything you can. Take notes on what you learn, and always jot down where the information came from.

The Wonderful Web

The Internet is another great place to gather information. People post government documents and **statistics** on sites. Podcasts have interviews with activists or experts. Videos can even give you a look at a place or event. Lots of youth activism networking sites are online too. These sites connect people with similar views. People on these sites help each other and share information. Check these sites out. There might be kids near you working toward the same goal. Just remember to be careful when you're online. Don't give out your personal information to people you don't know or trust.

Pounding the Pavement

Your research won't be complete until you start talking to people. Don't be afraid to call on the experts. These are people who know a lot about your issue. They might work for universities, government agencies, or organizations. If you're concerned about your drinking water, visit the water treatment plant. Worried about the trash in the landfills? Talk to waste management leaders.

When you did your reading or Web surfing, you probably came across some environmental activist organizations. There are hundreds of them out there. Get in touch with people involved with organizations. Ask them what their goals are and how they are working toward them. Tell these people about your ideas. They might have some helpful suggestions or new resources for you.

If your goal is to change or make a law, you'll have to talk with the people in charge. Phone numbers for your local, state, or national leaders are in your phone book and online. Give

these people a call. See if you can set up a time to talk in person. Tell them about your ideas for change. Listen to their thoughts about the topic too.

Question It

As you research, you will probably find information that says one thing and information that says the complete opposite. Some of the information out there is not meant to inform people. It's meant to **persuade** people. It's good to gather this type of information so you know what people are saying. But it's equally important to question that type of information. Why? Because information can be changed to support one point of view. Try asking these questions when you do your research.

Is the information coming from a trusted **source**? Universities and research centers provide solid information. But should you trust information you found on a blog? Remember, anyone can post things online. Double check the facts you get with other sources to be sure you have the best data.

Is the information based on stereotypes? When people use stereotypes, they assume all people in the group are exactly alike. If you see an article that says, "All politicians hate the environment," question it. Can you find a politician who works to help an environmental cause?

Does the information seem incomplete? Some people will leave out facts on purpose. They do this if the facts don't support their opinions. A really helpful piece of information will give all sides of a topic. If the facts you're getting seem one-sided, keep looking.

persuade — to change someone's opinion
source — someone or something that provides information

Otana Jakpor of Riverside, California, was looking for a science fair project. When this 13-year-old read an article about air purifiers, she had not only found her project, she got concerned.

The article Otana read said that some air purifiers put out large amounts of ozone gas. Ozone, also known as smog, can be harmful to people and animals. But Otana noticed that the article didn't include any research on the topic.

Otana designed three experiments to test the ozone levels of different air purifiers. One result was amazing. The level of ozone from the purifier was 15 times higher than the level of a stage 3 smog alert.

After her research, Otana learned the California Air Resources Board was working on a rule to limit the amount of ozone that came from purifiers. She sent the board her research. Otana's research was so thorough, it was used to support the rule. With Otana's information, the board made California the first state to limit ozone from purifiers.

Otana Jakpor

17

PLAN IT OUT

STEP 4: SET A GOAL AND MAKE A PLAN

You've picked a cause and thought about what to do. You've also researched a lot. It's now time for step 4 — making a plan of action. The very first thing you need to do is define your goal. What do you really want to do? On a piece of paper, write down your goal and what you hope to achieve. Just saying that you want to clean up the environment is too big. Be specific. If your goal is cleaning trash out of Spring Creek, everyone will understand your goal.

Once you have your goal ready, you'll need a plan of action. Step 4 is all about making plans. You don't want to take action without being prepared. Try to think of everything you'll need. If you're not sure what to do, ask others for help.

> *Tip* Don't be afraid to brainstorm big ideas. With help from others who care about your issue, you can accomplish big things.

As you're planning, ask yourself these questions:

- Who will you need to talk to for help? And how many people will you need to get the work done?
- What are you planning to do? Will you make posters to raise awareness about an endangered animal? Will you talk to politicians about a law to clean up air pollution?
- When are you going to start your action? How long will it take? If you're planning a big rally, your plan could take months. It's good to know up front that you could be planning this event for a long time.
- Where are you going to take action? Will you need permission from school administrators or community leaders?
- Why are you planning this course of action over another? Is your idea the best way to achieve your goal?
- How? Plan your action step-by-step. What items will you need, and what advertising will you do?

Tap into Your Talents

Think about skills you have as you make your plan. If you can't sing, holding a concert probably isn't the best way to raise money. But if you like to write, make a pamphlet or blog. Like talking? Ask teachers and clubs if you can make a presentation for them.

Is It Worth the Risk?

As you plan, remember that your actions could affect other people. If you're planning to **picket** outside a company that pollutes water, be prepared for the company's reaction. Its leaders probably won't agree with you. If you're planning to clean trash at a park, a city official might worry you'll get hurt. Before you take action, think about the risks involved.

Some risks will be okay to take. Questioning a company's practices is fine. Just don't be surprised if its leaders get upset. But if your plans are meant to hurt or cause trouble, you probably won't get the desired result. Risky plans scare people away. And you won't get them to join your cause. If you're not sure if the risks are worth taking, talk about your plan with other people. They can help you figure out if the plan will help you reach your goal.

picket – to stand outside a place to spread your message

Action Spotlight

At school, Angela Primbas learned that water pollution kills fish. Angela and her friends wondered if this was happening in Ohio, where they lived. So 12-year-old Angela and two of her friends spoke with public officials and park workers. They contacted wildlife experts and visited nature centers. They learned that pollution was slowly killing the brook trout that lived in local streams.

Angela and her friends formed a group called Save Our Stream (SOS). SOS set a goal to inform people about the brook trout and how they could help save the fish. The team's actions raised awareness and helped the fish population thrive.

But Angela didn't stop there. A couple of years later, she started a new group to stop pollution in Lake Erie. Angela and her group, Lake Kleenerz, led workshops for teachers, homeowners, and boaters. They taught people ways to stop pollution in Lake Erie.

Angela Primbas (middle)

CHAPTER 5

TAKE ACTION!

STEP 5: PUT YOUR PLAN INTO ACTION

You've got your plan. You've talked with others and thought everything through. Now make it happen. Start by getting other people to join you. Family and friends are a great place to start. Show them your plan, and answer their questions. Once they're on board, have some jobs ready for them. If you're starting a school club, ask your mom to speak with the principal with you. If your friend is a computer genius, have him make a Web site.

Next branch out and talk with people you don't know. Talk with kids at school about your ideas. Maybe you could make a presentation at your church. Call up your political leaders and ask them for help. Step 5 is all about getting out there and making things happen. Whatever you do, you're taking action!

Tip Always focus on the positive change you want to make. You'll come across as confident and optimistic. People will be more willing to support your cause.

Get Some Attention

Be visible. If you want to raise awareness about an issue, you'll need to speak out. But that doesn't necessarily mean you have to talk. You could design a T-shirt, a button, a wristband, or cap that promotes your cause. When you're out in public, wear it. If people ask you about your shirt, stop and talk to them. You never know where you'll find more help.

The media is another way to get the word out. Reporters and radio show hosts are always on the lookout for great stories. A young person with a plan to do something good makes a great story. Contact TV reporters, newspaper writers, and even the local radio station. You might become the latest news feature.

Respect

As you get more and more attention, you might hear many more opinions. Not everyone will support your cause. That's okay. Be respectful of those other points of view. You don't have to agree, but you do want to be polite. You'll always gain more support for yourself and your cause if you treat others with respect.

Action Spotlight

When Zander Srodes was 11 years old, he spent weekends on the beach in Florida. Zander and his friends pointed flashlights at the sea turtles nesting there and left toys in the sand at night. Then a local teacher explained to Zander that his actions could actually hurt the animals.

Zander wondered if other kids knew that. He decided to make sure they learned. To start, he went to a nearby marine laboratory and learned everything he could about sea turtles. Then he created an education program called "Turtle Talks." Zander told kids about the turtles and their young. And he taught them about how pollution hurts the animals. Zander even brought a turtle costume for kids to wear.

As his "Turtle Talks" became more popular, Zander expanded his efforts. He wrote and published two books. More than 5,000 children have learned about the endangered sea turtle thanks to Zander.

Zander Srodes

Every Step Makes Change

It is not an easy thing to make change. You can expect to spend a lot of time working toward your goal. But it will be worth it!

There is always a chance that you won't achieve your goal. The company you fought against might continue to dump waste in the lake. The ditch you cleaned might become littered again. But don't let that discourage you. Every single step you take makes a difference. Maybe you changed just one person's mind about pollution. Maybe you got three families to recycle. That's action!

And you don't have to stop. If you reach your goal, or even if you don't, keep working. You can always go back to the list you made in step 1. Tackle a new issue that you care about. Or maybe you'll keep working on the same issue. You can make a new plan, talk to different people, and take action in a new way. This world is yours. If you don't like something, you have the power to make change. Making big change takes time and effort. But one step at a time, you can do it!

RESOURCES

There are hundreds of resources that can help you be an environmentalist. Below is a short list to help you get started in your research. But don't stop with this list. Find your own resources that will help you reach your goal.

Clean Air Task Force

The Clean Air Task Force is focused on cleaning up the air and creating a healthier environment for everyone. Members on the CATF include scientists, lawyers, and economists. Members work with state and national lawmakers to bring attention to clean air policies. The CATF Web site outlines projects members are currently working on.

Earthwatch Institute

The Earthwatch Institute focuses its work on scientific research and education to help people understand how to protect the earth. Earthwatch funds scientists who research a variety of environmental issues. The organization also offers programs to students and teachers. With Web-based expeditions, Earthwatch educates students around the world about the earth and the problems it faces.

The Freechild Project

The Freechild Project is a program that provides tools, training, and advice to youth activists. The project's Web site offers information on a variety of issues and actions. There are many free resources and ideas for youth to use to work toward change in their worlds.

Greenpeace

Greenpeace is an international organization dedicated to protecting the environment. With offices in more than 30 countries, Greenpeace activists address threats that concern the planet. The organization's Web site offers many ideas on getting involved, as well as information on topics from global warming to nuclear energy.

National Recycling Coalition

The National Recycling Coalition is dedicated to promoting recycling on the local, state, and federal levels. The NRC works to improve recycling, reduce waste, and promote composting. The NRC's Web site also offers information about state and local recycling organizations. This information provides people with a way to reach leaders in their area.

Sierra Club

The Sierra Club is the oldest environmental organization in the United States. The club is dedicated to protecting the earth's wilderness areas. Members also work to educate others about using natural resources responsibly and protecting the environment.

WireTap Magazine

WireTap is an online magazine for young people who want to create social change. The focus is on news and culture. Topics covered include the environment, politics, racial justice, war and peace, and education.

World Wildlife Fund

The World Wildlife Fund is focused on protecting natural areas and the plants and animals that live there. Experts with WWF work to protect endangered species on planet earth. WWF's more than 5 million members come from 100 countries around the world.

Glossary

brainstorm (BRAYN-storm) – to think of many ideas without judging them as good or bad

cause (KAWZ) – an aim or principle for which people believe in and work

extinct (ik-STINGKT) – no longer living; an extinct animal is one that has died out with no more of its kind.

persuade (pur-SWADE) – to succeed in making someone do or believe something

picket (PIK-it) – to stand outside a place to spread your message

source (SORSS) – someone or something that provides information

statistic (stuh-TISS-tik) – a fact shown as a number or percentage

stereotype (STER-ee-oh-tipe) – an overly simple opinion of a person, group, or thing

Read More

Botzakis, Stergios. *What's Your Source?: Questioning the News.* Media Literacy. Mankato, Minn.: Capstone Press, 2009.

Hoose, Phillip. *It's Our World, Too!: Young People Who Are Making a Difference: How They Do It – How YOU Can, Too!* New York: Farrar, Straus and Giroux, 2002.

Lewis, Barbara A. *The Teen Guide to Global Action: How to Connect with Others (Near and Far) to Create Social Change.* Minneapolis: Free Spirit, 2008.

Internet Sites

FactHound offers a safe, fun way to find educator-approved Internet sites related to this book.

Here's what you do:

1. Visit *www.facthound.com*

2. Choose your grade level.

3. Begin your search.

This book's ID number is 9781429627979.

FactHound will fetch the best sites for you!

Index

Meet the Author

Mary McIntyre Coley is a lifelong nature lover. She has worked as a water education specialist, an outreach director for the Oklahoma chapter of a conservation organization, a writer, a naturalist, and a park planner, all in her home state of Oklahoma. Currently, she is a communications officer for the city of Tulsa, specializing in environmental topics.

Meet the Consultant

Adam Fletcher is a private consultant who has worked with thousands of youth and adults, teaching them how to share their energy and wisdom with each other. He started The Freechild Project to share resources with kids on how to change the world. He also created SoundOut to teach people in schools how to listen to student voice.